BECAUSE HE LIVES

Words and Music by WILLIAM J. GAITHER
and GLORIA GAITHER
Arranged by John Purifoy

With great feeling (♩= ca. 78)

With pedal

PIANO SOLO

Sacred Classics

FOR SOLO PIANO

ARRANGED BY JOHN PURIFOY

ISBN 978-1-4950-1043-9

HAL•LEONARD®
CORPORATION
7777 W. BLUEMOUND RD. P.O. BOX 13819 MILWAUKEE, WI 53213

Visit Hal Leonard Online at
www.halleonard.com

FOREWORD

As I finished the last title for this collection, it hit me that I remember when almost every single piece was brand-new!

I was a twenty-something music editor when 2nd Chapter of Acts recorded "Easter Song," and youth choirs and churches everywhere were singing it in the '70s. Later in the decade, Sandi Patty launched her vocal career with "We Shall Behold Him." Bill and Gloria Gaither's worship musical, *Alleluia*, featured a congregational chorus entitled "Because He Lives," which became an immediate standard in hymnals of all denominations.

As I arranged each piece, I remembered these times and worship experiences that shaped my own journey and still resonate deeply today. I hope that as you play these settings—whether at home, with friends or in worship—they will do the same. Music will always have that transcending quality to connect memories, times and places to the sacred moment that is now.

With gratitude,

John Purifoy

EASTER SONG

Words and Music by
ANNE HERRING
Arranged by John Purifoy

With growing energy! ($\quarternote$ = ca. 144)

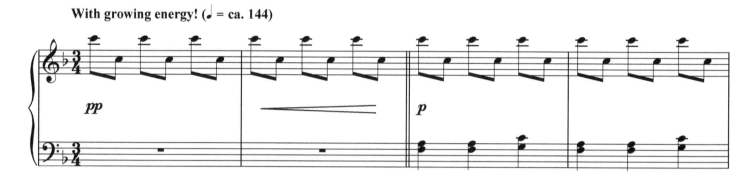

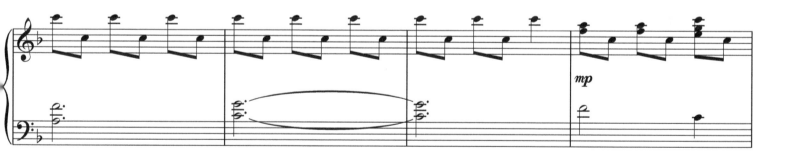

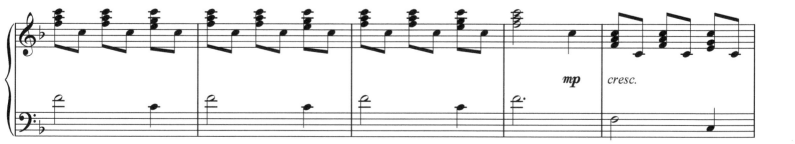

GLORIFY THY NAME

Words and Music by
DONNA W. ADKINS
Arranged by John Purifoy

Smoothly, with expression (♩ = ca. 96)

Slower

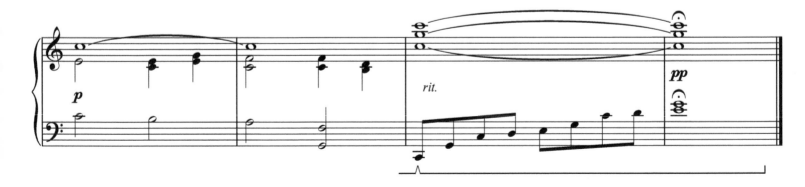

MAJESTY

Words and Music by
JACK HAYFORD
Arranged by John Purifoy

Reverently, with growing purpose (♩ = ca. 96)

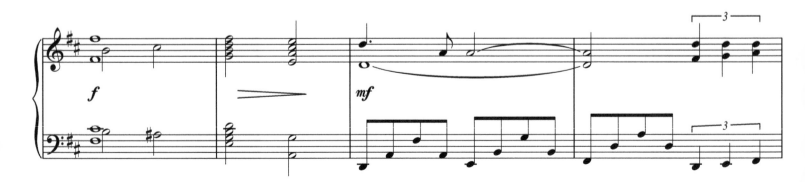

HERE AM I, SEND ME

Words and Music by
JOHN PURIFOY
Arranged by John Purifoy

Smoothly, with expression (♩ = ca. 96)

mp

Pedal harmonically

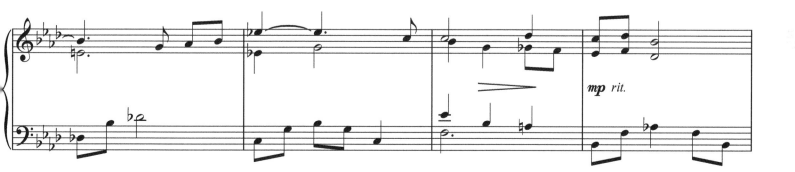

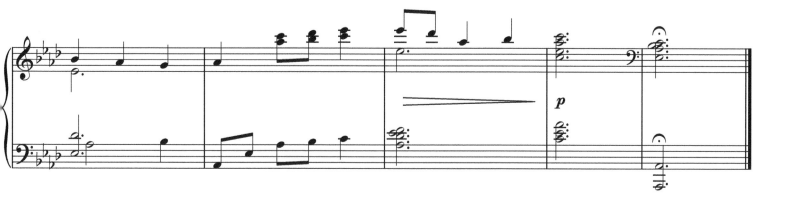

I'D RATHER HAVE JESUS

Words by RHEA F. MILLER
Music by GEORGE BEVERLY SHEA
Arranged by John Purifoy

With reverence and freedom (♩ = ca. 88)

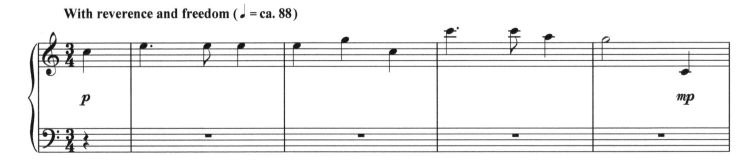

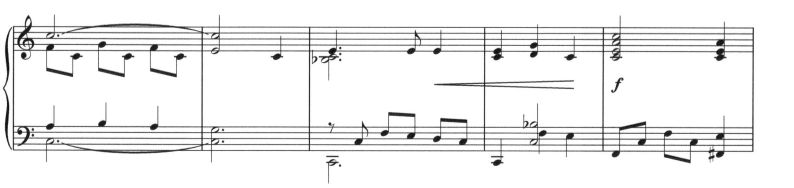

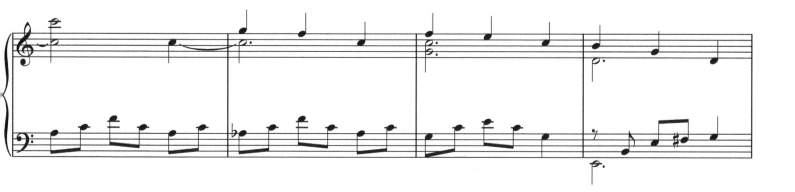

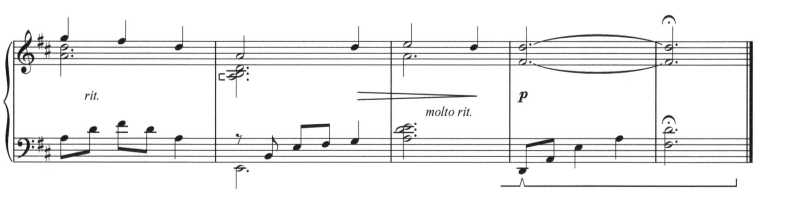

ON EAGLE'S WINGS

Words and Music by
MICHAEL JONCAS
Arranged by John Purifoy

With much freedom (♩ = ca. 88)

Pedal harmonically

rit. poco a poco

a tempo

mf

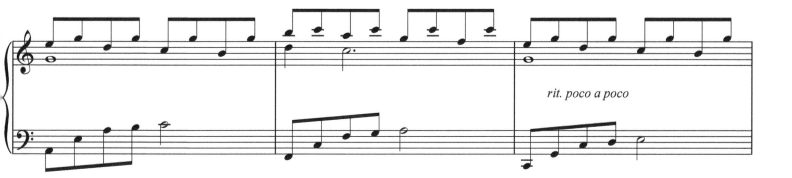

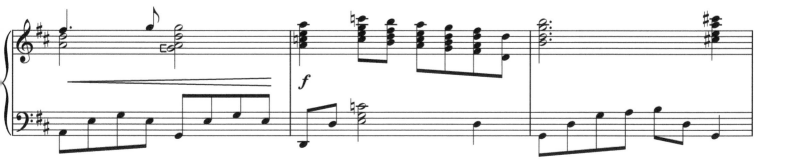

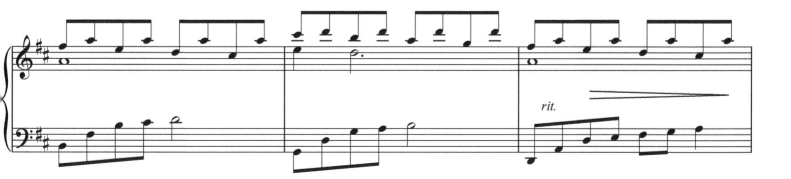

WE SHALL BEHOLD HIM

Words and Music by
DOTTIE RAMBO
Arranged by John Purifoy

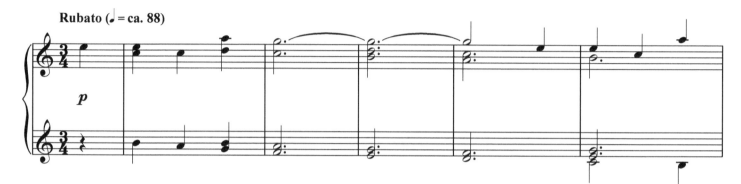

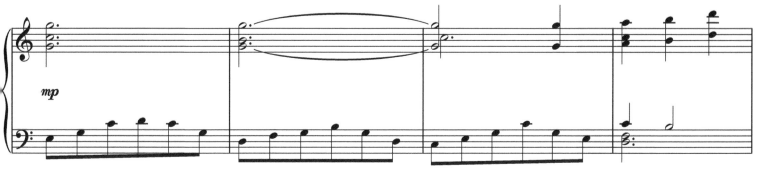

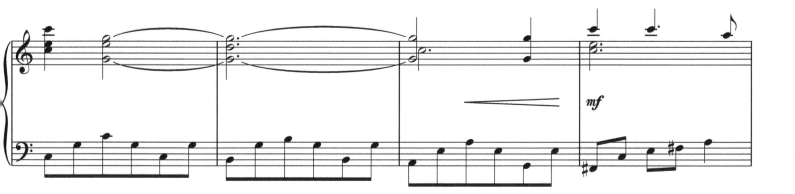

In tempo, with movement (♩ = ca. 92)

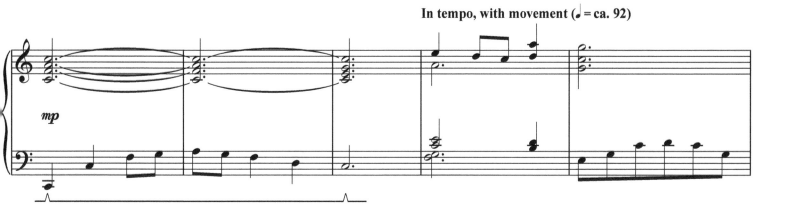

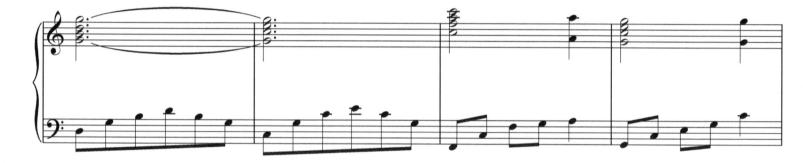

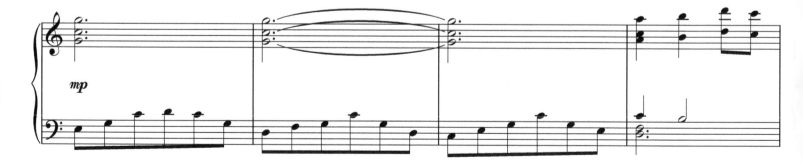

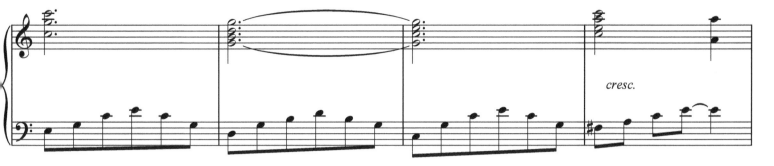

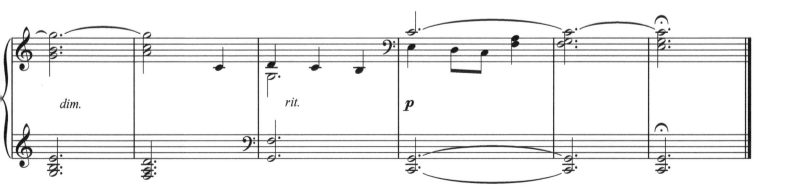

WORTHY IS THE LAMB

Text Based on Revelation 5:12
Adapted by DON WYRTZEN
Music by DON WYRTZEN
Arranged by John Purifoy

Steadily, with purpose (♩ = ca. 88)

mp

With pedal

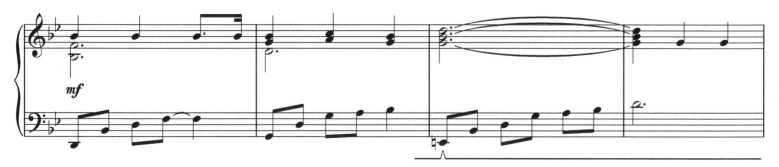

mf

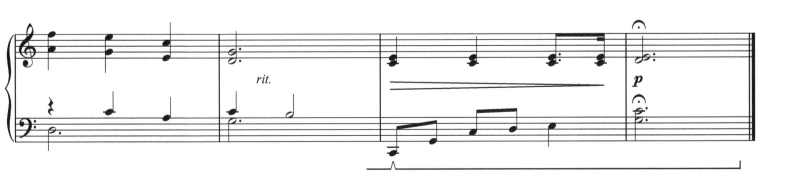

THERE'S SOMETHING ABOUT THAT NAME

Words by WILLIAM J. and GLORIA GAITHER
Music by WILLIAM J. GAITHER
Arranged by John Purifoy

Gently, with expression (♩=ca. 88)

mp

Pedal harmonically

rit.

a tempo

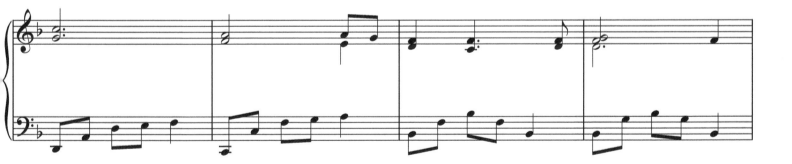